A Pride of Lions

Heinemann Library
Chicago, Illinois

Richard and Louise Spilsbury

Customer Service 888-454-2279
Visit our website at www.heinemannlibrary.com

Designed by Ron Kamen and Celia Floyd
Originated by Dot Gradations Ltd
Printed in Hong Kong, China by Wing King Tong

07 06 05 04 03
10 9 8 7 6 5 4 3 2 1

Library of Congress Cataloging-in-Publication Data
Spilsbury, Louise.
  A pride of lions / Louise and Richard Spilsbury.
    v. cm. -- (Animal groups)
Contents: What are lions? -- What is a pride like? -- Where do prides live? -- What happens in a pride? -- How do lions hunt? -- Do prides hunt together? -- How do lions care for their young? -- How do lions communicate? -- Do prides change? -- What dangers threaten prides?
  ISBN 1-4034-0745-2 (HC)   1-4034-3287-2 (PB)
  1. Lions--Juvenile literature. [1. Lions.] I. Spilsbury, Richard, 1963- II. Title. III. Series.
  QL737.C23 S588 2003
  599.757--dc21
                    2002004019

Acknowledgments
The author and publishers are grateful to the following for permission to reproduce copyright material:
p. 4 Hilary Pooley/Oxford Scientific Films; p. 5 Ann and Steve Toon/NHPA; p. 6 Still Pictures; pp. 7, 17 Andy Rouse/NHPA; p. 8 John Shaw/NHPA; p. 9 Nigel J. Dennis/NHPA; pp. 10, 18 Anup Shah (BBC Wild)/Nature Picture Library; pp. 11, 14 Anthony Bannister/NHPA; pp. 13, 23 (bottom) Steve Bloom; p. 15 John Downer/Oxford Scientific Films; p. 16 J. and A. Scott/NHPA; p. 19 Stan Osolinski/Oxford Scientific Films; p. 20 National Geographic; p. 21 Philip Perry/FLPA; p. 22 Bruce Coleman Collection; pp. 23 (top), 25 Minden Pictures/FLPA; p. 24 Rafi Ben-Shanar/Oxford Scientific Films; p. 26 Martin Harvey/NHPA; p. 27 Diego Lezama Orezzoli/Corbis; p. 28 Daryl Balfour/NHPA.

Cover photograph of an African lioness and cubs, reproduced with permission of Bruce Coleman Collection/Erwin and Peggy Bauer.

The publishers would like to thank Claire Robinson for her assistance in the preparation of this book.

Every effort has been made to contact copyright holders of any material reproduced in this book. Any omissions will be rectified in subsequent printings if notice is given to the publisher.

Some words are shown in bold, **like this.** You can find out what they mean by looking in the glossary.

Contents

Lions are large, powerful cats with long bodies and tails. They are covered in short, thick fur that is mostly the same yellowish-brown color all over. The only parts that are a different color are their undersides, which are often paler, and the back of their ears and tips of their tails, which are black. Lions are the only cats that have a tuft, or fluffy end, to their tails.

Male and female

When fully grown, male lions are bigger than female lions, which are called lionesses. What makes them really easy to tell apart is the male's **mane**. This is a thick collar of longer fur that surrounds a male's face and neck. It makes the male look even bigger than he is. As a male gets older, his mane gets darker.

The lion is often called the "king of the beasts," because it is so large and strong. Its mighty roar can be heard far and wide.

What Are Cats?

There are 37 different **species** of wild cats in the world. Most are a lot like pet cats. They have round heads with large eyes, upright ears, and long whiskers near their mouths. Many cats have patterned fur and soft padded paws. Tigers, leopards, and cheetahs are other species of big cats. When people talk about "big cats," they mean large wild cats.

Groups of lions

Most kinds of cats live, hunt, and sleep alone. Lions are unusual cats because they live in groups. Even though you may see a lion alone, it is still part of a group, and it returns to its group at some point. A group of lions is called a pride.

A lion can be about three feet (one meter) tall and measure over nine feet (three meters) from nose to tail—about the length of a small car!

What Is a Pride Like?

A pride of lions usually includes about fifteen lions, but some may have as many as 40 members. Most of the lions in a pride are females and their young, along with two or three adult males.

The female lions in a pride are usually related. This is because lionesses tend to stay in the pride into which they are born. The young males move away when they are two or three years old. The pride is mostly made up of sisters, aunts, mothers, and grandmothers who have all grown up together. One of the reasons lion prides work so well is because the females have been together for a long time, they know and trust each other.

Although prides vary, a pride of lions often includes about two males, five lionesses, four young lions, and three babies.

Alone and in groups

The whole pride is not together very often. Most of the time, the male lions go around alone or with other males from the pride. The female lions spend their time in small groups with other females and their **cubs**, or babies. These groups may change every day as lions spend time with different members of the pride.

Different roles in a pride

Male and female lions have different jobs in the pride. The females do most of the hunting. They get most of the food for themselves and the other lions in the pride. They also take care of the cubs. The males are the protectors of the pride. Their job is to keep the place where the pride lives safe from enemies.

A male lion's mane makes him look big and strong and helps him scare off lions from other prides.

7

Where Do Prides of Lions Live?

Most prides of lions live in Africa. In the past, lions also lived throughout India, the Middle East, and southern Asia. People have killed many of these lions or taken over their **habitats** for human use. Today, the only place you can find wild lions outside Africa is in one **national park** in India.

Lions live in habitats called **savanna** or **scrub.** These places have a long, hot dry season and a shorter season when heavy rain falls. There is a scattering of a few trees and thorny bushes. Sometimes there is even a small forest. But it is too hot and dry for many large plants to grow. Lions prefer to live among big patches of dry grass where there are good views of the animals they hunt.

The dry grasses of the savanna are the same yellowish-brown color as most lions' fur. This **camouflage** helps lions hide among the grasses while they are hunting.

8

How Large Is a Pride's Territory?

In places where there are lots of **prey**, a pride's **territory** is smaller than in an area where there are fewer animals to hunt. Some prides have territories that are over 96 square miles (250 square kilometers) in size to be sure there is enough food for all the pride members.

A pride's patch

A pride of lions always lives in a particular area within their habitat, which is called their territory. They choose an area where plenty of prey live, such as gazelles, buffalo, zebra, and antelope, so there is enough food for all the pride. Most territories also contain a **watering hole**—a lake or river where there is always water. In such a hot habitat, lions can die if they do not drink enough water.

Lions come to watering holes like this to drink and to catch other thirsty animals that visit.

Guarding the territory

Adult male lions spend a lot of their time guarding the pride's **territory**. They want to keep other lions out because they might take the pride's food. The males walk around their territory in groups, like guards. If they find an animal that has strayed into their territory, the males may try to kill it.

Scent Marks

● ● ● ● ● ● ● ● ● ●

Male lions often spray their strong-smelling **urine** onto trees, bushes, stones, or paths inside their pride's territory. These are called **scent marks**. They tell other lions that the territory belongs to the pride. By sniffing, other lions can tell how long ago a male passed by and can guess how safe it would be to walk through the territory.

One way males mark their territory is by scuffing the ground with their claws. They scratch away at the ground with their back feet and spray urine there, too.

What Happens in a Pride?

If you look around a pride's territory during the daytime, you probably won't see much. Lions spend most of their time asleep, resting, or **grooming**. They usually lie out in the open or under the shade of a tree. But they are hard to spot because of their **camouflaged** fur. They become more active in the early evening. This is when the young **cubs** play and **suckle** from their mothers. This is also the time when the adult lions hunt for food.

When groups of lionesses relax, they often stretch out with their heads, legs, and tails draped over each other.

Grooming

When animals lick and clean each other, they are grooming. Lionesses do most of the grooming in a pride. They groom each other as well as the cubs and males. Grooming keeps the lions clean and makes everyone feel like part of the pride.

Active lions

Adult lions may spend a lot of their active time walking around. They may walk about five miles (eight kilometers) each day, searching for **prey**. When they find prey, it takes a lot of strength to catch and kill it. This is why lions rest a lot during the day. They are saving their energy for hunting.

Feasting

Prides do not usually kill prey to eat every day. They are more likely to catch food every two or three days. After eating a really big meal, the pride may spend the next day or so just resting and letting their bodies **digest** the food. They don't need to hunt if their stomachs are full, and the extra weight also means they cannot run as fast.

What Do Lions Eat?

Lions are **carnivores**, which means they eat other animals. Lions prefer to eat large animals that eat grass, or **grazers**, such as wildebeest, zebra, antelope, and buffalo. Sometimes they even hunt young giraffes and elephants. If they cannot catch big animals, they eat smaller ones, such as warthogs, hares, and tortoises. If food is really scarce, lions will eat almost anything, including snakes, insects, or fruit.

The fact that a pride always lives in the same **territory** means that when the lions go hunting at night, they know where the best places are to find food.

13

How Do Lions Catch Their Food?

Lions are good at catching animals for food. They have strong **muscles** in their chest and front legs for grabbing large **prey** and pulling it to the ground. A lion's paws have sharp, curved claws that can hook into an animal's skin. Then its strong jaws clamp around the animal's throat to kill it.

Lions usually hunt at dawn or dusk so they can sneak up on prey. Lions have excellent **senses** of hearing and sight. They can hear prey almost one mile (two kilometers) away and twist their ears to pinpoint the source of a sound. Their golden eyes see at night almost as well as human eyes can see during the daytime!

A lion has 30 teeth. It uses its four pointed **canine** teeth to hold prey and tear off meat to eat. Its other teeth bite through tough skin. Lions do not need to have teeth for chewing, because they swallow chunks of meat whole.

If a prey animal looks up while a lion is hunting it, the lion will stand still to avoid being seen.

Stalking and jumping

Lions are too heavy to run quickly for long. Most of their prey can run faster than they can. This is why lions **stalk** their prey. At first, they move slowly and quietly toward the prey, keeping low to the ground and hiding behind plants. They watch the prey carefully the entire time. When they are close enough, they rush out and jump on the prey.

Stealing Food

To avoid the hard work of hunting, lions often **scavenge**, or steal food killed by other animals. Lions can tell there is **carrion** nearby when there are vultures circling in the sky or hyenas calling. These animals are good at finding **carrion**, so lions can follow them to a free meal.

15

Do Lions Hunt Together?

The lionesses usually hunt the food for a pride. By hunting together they can catch more **prey.** They can also combine their strength to catch much bigger animals than they could alone.

Lionesses often split into smaller groups when hunting. Different lionesses have different jobs in the hunt. Larger, heavier lionesses wait to catch running prey. Faster, lighter lionesses chase it toward them.

When they attack a herd of prey animals, lionesses often go for the younger or weaker members because they run more slowly.

Ways of hunting

Sometimes lionesses form a line and chase prey into a dead end, such as a **watering hole.** The chased animals panic and try to run back the way they came, straight toward the waiting lions. At other times, lionesses form a wide circle around a herd of prey and close in on it.

Lazy Males?

Male lions usually trail behind the lionesses when they hunt. They don't take part in chasing and catching prey, but as soon as an animal is caught, they run up and demand to eat first. They end up eating the most. A male lion can eat 75 pounds (34 kilograms) of meat in one meal.

Mealtime fights

When the hunters have caught an animal, the other lions in the pride run up. Male lions eat first, but the females complain angrily until they get a turn. **Cubs** have to wait until last. It is quite common for lion cubs to starve to death in their first year because they cannot get enough food.

At mealtimes, lions growl and snap at each other. If the other lions did not make such a fuss, the males might go on eating until there was nothing left.

Does the Pride Care for the Cubs?

When a lioness becomes an adult, she can **mate** with the older males in the pride. Her **cubs** are born about fourteen weeks later. Lionesses usually have three or four cubs at a time. At first, the cubs are small and helpless. They are blind for the first two weeks and cannot run for a month, so the mothers have to take good care of them.

Lions' lairs

Lions do not make homes that they live in all the time, but when they have cubs, lionesses keep them in **lairs.** A lair is any place where the cubs can be well hidden from hyenas, leopards, and other **predators.** It could be a space between some bushes or fallen trees, or a dip in the ground.

Mothers move their cubs from one lair to another to keep them safe. They carry the cubs gently by the neck.

Growing up in a pride

One of the reasons lions live in a pride is so the cubs are well cared for. A mother lion may leave her cubs for whole days and nights while she hunts or relaxes with other lions from the pride. The cubs survive because they can **suckle** from any of the lionesses with cubs in their pride. These other lionesses also act as baby-sitters, looking after the cubs while their mother is away.

Watch and learn

Young cubs in a pride learn a lot from watching what the older lions do. They also learn as they play, because they are practicing skills they will need when they are older. For example, when a mother lion flicks her tail for her cub to chase, the cub is learning how to jump on fast-moving **prey**.

Young cubs practice fighting with other cubs as there is no chance of being badly hurt.

19

Do Lions Talk to Each Other?

When humans want to tell someone something, we can **communicate** it in different ways. Besides talking, we send messages using our face and body. For example, frowning, smiling, pointing, or waving all send a certain message. Lions have different ways of communicating, too. They tell other lions how they feel or pass on information using sound, movement, scent, or touch.

Sounds lions make

Lions make at least nine different sounds, including growls, snarls, and meows. Different sounds mean different things. The most familiar lion sound is the roar, which can be heard up to six miles (nine kilometers) away. Lions usually roar in the evening or after feeding. The roar reminds lions who don't belong to the pride who the **territory** belongs to. It warns them to keep out!

When pride members roar together, it tells lions from other prides to keep away. It also makes the lions in the pride feel more like a team.

Soft and loud

Lions can make each of their sounds louder or softer, depending on what they want to communicate. When mothers call their **cubs**, they make low, quiet grunting sounds. Cubs meow to greet their mothers and purr when they are calm and happy. The lionesses use slightly louder grunts to keep in touch with each other when they are out hunting, especially when it is dark.

Body language

Lions use body language, through body movements and positions, to communicate how they feel. A flicking tail and head kept low mean that the lion is thinking of attacking. When young lions hold their mouths open without showing their teeth, they want to play. Lions show their teeth to let others know they are angry or ready to attack.

A lion's black lips, ear backs, and tail tuft make any movements of these parts more obvious. This lioness's partly open mouth, stiff tail, and pricked ears signal to others that she has spotted possible **prey**.

21

Keeping the pride together

Most of the time, the lions in a pride get along well. They often show that they like each other. They do this by sitting or lying close together, rubbing against each other, **grooming**, and licking one another's faces. Doing these things helps to keep the members of the pride together and reminds them they are all part of a team or family.

The Greeting Ceremony

When members of a pride meet, they always greet each other in the same way. First they sniff each other's noses, then they moan softly, rub heads, then sides, and drape their tails across each other's backs. It's sort of like the way we kiss or hug our families to say we are happy to see them.

The greeting ceremony is an important way for lions to prove to each other that they belong to the same pride.

Lions use smell as a way of identifying pride members. Because they are always grooming, rubbing heads, and licking each other, the lions in a pride smell alike.

Lions from the same pride sometimes fight, especially over food. To stop the fight, the weaker of the two lions may lie on its back. This says to the stronger lion, "I give up," and the fight stops.

Do Prides Change?

A pride stays together for a long time, but every few years, there is a change. Female members of a pride stay together for many years, but all young males leave their prides when they are between two and three years old.

Why do males leave?

The older males—the father lions—often chase the young males out of the pride. These males form a gang. They wander around together for several years until they are old enough and strong enough to take over a pride of their own. To do this, they get the adult male lions of that pride to fight. If they win, they will take over the pride and its **territory.**

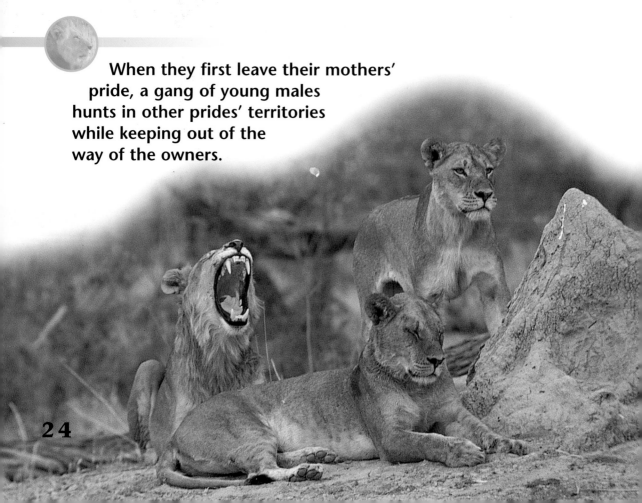

When they first leave their mothers' pride, a gang of young males hunts in other prides' territories while keeping out of the way of the owners.

After a male leader of a pride is beaten in a fight, he is often badly hurt and may die. Sometimes he escapes, but he will not be able to return to the pride.

Running a pride

Males usually control a pride when they are at their strongest, around five or six years old. Most adult males only get to control a pride for between two and three years. After this, they are weaker, so when younger males try to take over their pride, they lose the fight.

Cub Killing

When new male lions take over a pride, they usually kill all the **cubs** they find there. This may seem cruel, but they do this so that the females are ready to **mate** with them sooner. Usually, lionesses can only have new cubs when their other cubs are nearly two. If they lose cubs, they can mate a few days later. This means the new leaders become the fathers of all the cubs in the pride. This is why all the cubs in a pride are about the same age.

What Dangers Does a Pride Face?

Living in a pride protects lions from many dangers. The fact that lions usually stay in a group means that they have hardly any **predators**. If a lion is hurt, it can still eat meat the others have caught until it is well again. If a lioness is killed, other lionesses in the pride care for her **cubs**.

Lions at risk

Of all lions, cubs are in the most danger. Leopards, hyenas, and male lions from other prides try to catch and eat young cubs. Other lions can be hurt or killed while catching **prey**. A zebra, giraffe, or buffalo may kick them or a snake or crocodile may bite them. Lions try to kill their prey quickly, before they can get hurt.

Hyenas work in teams, and can kill an adult lion if it is hurt. If food is scarce, hyenas may even fight with a healthy lion over some **carrion**.

Do Lions Attack People?

Lions do sometimes attack people, but it is unusual. An old lion with worn teeth or one that has been hurt may kill and eat a person because a human is easier to catch than faster prey. But most of the time, lions try to avoid people because people have weapons that can kill them.

Because lions live in open areas, hunters and herders can hunt them easily.

People are a pride's greatest threat

The greatest threat to any pride is humans. Farmers and **herders** kill many lions each year. They do this because lions can kill and eat farm animals, such as cattle, that belong to them. Some countries still allow hunters to shoot lions for sport. This can greatly damage a pride, because hunters usually try to kill the biggest males. If they kill a leader male from a pride, the pride will then be taken over by a new male, who will kill all the cubs.

27

Nowhere to live, nothing to eat

The other way humans are a danger to lions is by destroying the **habitats** in which lions live. In Africa, people are taking over much of the land to build farms and towns. When there are fewer areas of grass for **grazers** like zebras to feed on, they die. Grazers are a lion's main **prey**, so prides of lions gradually starve and die if there are not enough animals for them to eat.

Protecting prides

Many African countries are working hard to protect lions. They set up areas where no one is allowed to use land for building or farming. These protected areas are called **national parks** or **reserves**, and in them prides of lions can live in a safe and protected environment.

This pride of lions lives in the safety of the Chobe National Park in Africa.

Lion Facts

Where do lions live?

This map shows where most of the lions in the world live today. Around 300 Asian lions live in the Gir Forest National Park in Gujarat, western India, which is marked on the map. Lions live from fifteen to twenty years.

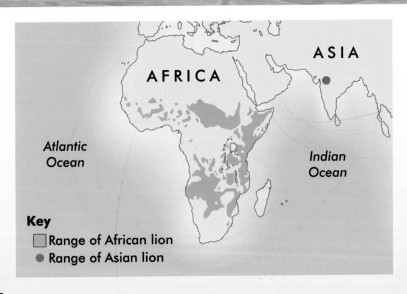

ASIA

AFRICA

Atlantic
Ocean

Indian
Ocean

Key
◻ Range of African lion
● Range of Asian lion

Getting around

Lions usually walk slowly. When they hunt, they can run up to 37 miles (60 kilometers) per hour, but only for a short distance. Lions are not great tree climbers, so they do lie on large, low branches.

Amazing vision

Lions can see well in the dark because they have a special layer in their eyes. If even a tiny amount of light gets into their eyes, this layer reflects it around inside their eyes so they can see.

Lion cubs

When lion **cubs** are born they weigh about three pounds (1.4 kilograms). Their fur is spotted at first as **camouflage**, to help them hide from **predators**. They drink milk from the mothers in the pride until they are about seven months old. Then they are ready to feed on meat with the other lions. They join in hunts when they are about eleven months old.

Glossary

camouflage colors and patterns that help an animal's body blend in with its background

canine long pointed teeth at the front of an animal's mouth

carnivore animal that mostly eats other animals

carrion meat from an animal that is already dead. Often the meat has begun to rot.

communicate pass information to one another

cub baby lion

digest break down food inside the body so it can be absorbed

grazer animal that eats grass or other plants. Grazers, such as zebra, usually live in herds.

grooming when animals lick or clean themselves or each other

habitat place where an animal or plant lives in the wild

herder person who takes groups of animals to a place where they can feed on plants

lair place where lion cubs can be well hidden, such as a space between some bushes or fallen trees

mane collar of fur around an adult male lion's neck

mate joining of a male and female of the same species to create young

muscle part of the body that helps to make the bones in the body move

national park area that is protected by law, so that people cannot harm the plants and animals that live there

predator animal that hunts other animals for food

prey animal that is hunted and eaten by another animal

reserve protected area where animals can live safely

savanna large, open area of land mostly covered in grasses but with patches of woodland

scavenge steal food from other animals

scent marks strong-smelling urine an animal has sprayed somewhere as a signal to other animals

scrub areas with sandy soil that have patches of trees and shrubs

sense animals have some or all of the following senses: hearing, sight, touch, smell, and taste

species group of living things that are alike in many ways and can mate to produce young

stalk quietly sneak up on an animal in order to get close enough to catch it

suckle when a baby animal drinks its mother's milk

territory particular area that an animal or group of animals claims as its own

urine liquid waste produced by animals' bodies

watering hole place where animals often go to drink water

More Books to Read

Clutton-Brock, Juliet. *Eyewitness: Cat.* New York: DK Publishing, 2000.

Corrigan, Patricia (Ed.). *Big Cats!* Chanhassen, Minn.: NorthWord Press, 2002.

Jordan, Bill. *Lion.* Austin, Tex.: Raintree Publishers, 1999.

Kalman, Bobbie. *The Life Cycle of a Lion.* New York: Crabtree Publishing, 2002.

Klevansk, Rhonda. *Nature Watch Big Cats.* Chicago: Lorenz Books, 1999.

Richardson, Adele D. *Lions.* Mankato, Minn.: Bridgestone Books, 2001.

Robinson, Claire. *Lions.* Chicago: Heinemann Library, 2001.

Winner, Cherie. *Lions.* Chanhassen, Minn.: NorthWord Press, 2001.

Index